THE WOLF WHO WANTED MY PANTS COLORING BOOK

By: Zylee and Karyann Villalobos

Copyright © 2020 by Zylee and Karyann Villalobos

All rights reserved. No part of this book may be reproduced or used in any manner without written permission of the copyright owners except for the use of quotations in a book review or for educational purposes.

www.ingramcontent.com/pod-product-compliance
Lightning Source LLC
Chambersburg PA
CBHW081130080526
44587CB00021B/3826